DISCARD

OCT 2016

DISCARD

Well Made, Fair Trade

My T-Shirt
and Other Clothing

W9-BUI-500

CRABTREE
Publishing Company
www.crabtreebooks.com

Crabtree Publishing Company
www.crabtreebooks.com
1-800-387-7650

Published in Canada
Crabtree Publishing
616 Welland Avenue
St. Catharines, ON
L2M 5V6

Published in the United States
Crabtree Publishing
PMB 59051
350 Fifth Ave, 59th Floor
New York, NY 10118

Author: Helen Greathead

Editorial director: Kathy Middleton

Editors: Julia Bird and Ellen Rodger

Designer: Q2A Media

Proofreader: Wendy Scavuzzo

Prepress technician: Margaret Amy Salter

Print and production coordinator: Katherine Berti

Published by Crabtree Publishing Company in 2017

All rights reserved. No part of this publication may be reproduced, stored in a retrieval system, or transmitted in any form or by any means, electronic, mechanical, photocopy, recording or otherwise, without the prior written permission of the copyright owner.

First published in 2015 by Franklin Watts
(A division of Hachette Children's Books)
Copyright © Franklin Watts 2015

Printed in Canada/072016/PB20160525

Photographs:
Front Cover: Elena Rostunova, Pressmaster, S1001, Africa Studio, Milosz_G/Shutterstock.
Back Cover: Photobank.ch/Shutterstock. Title Page: Alhovik, Karkas, Robert_s, Loukia, Bohbeh/Shutterstock.
Imprint Page: Africa Studio/Shutterstock. P4(R): Artjazz/Shutterstock, P4(TL): Mike Flippo/Shutterstock, P4(BL): Mike Flippo/Shutterstock, P4(CL): Urfin/Shutterstock; P5(TL): Fairtrade Organic, P5(B): Ekler/Shutterstock, P5(CR): Urfin/Shutterstock, P5(TR): Mike Flippo/Shutterstock, P5(C): Flas100/Shutterstock; P6 Mandy Godbehear/Shutterstock; P7: Lizette Potgieter/Shutterstock; P8(B): 2001–2014 People Tree and others, P8(T) Fairtrade Organic,P8(BKGRD): Surrphoto/Shutterstock; P9(TL): TongChuwit/Shutterstock, P9(C): Rapanui Clothing, P9(B): Rapanui Clothing, P9(TR): Q2a Media; P10–11(BKGRD): Flas100/Shutterstock, P10(C): 2014 LS&CO, P10(B): Nikonova Margarita/Shutterstock; P11(L): Africa Studio/Shutterstock, P11(R): Halina Yakushevich/Shutterstock; P12(T):WarOnWant.org, P12(BR): Kevin Rijnders/Kuyichi; P12–13(BKGRD): My Life Graphic/shutterstock, P13(B): Andrew Biraj/Reuters; P14(L): Aleksandra Zaitseva/Shutterstock, P14(R): Amorfati.art/Shutterstock; P15(T): Foto76/Shutterstock, P15(B): Sigit Pamungkas/Reuters; P14–15(BKGRD): Antonio Villani/Fotolia; P16–17(BKGRD): Antonio Villani/Fotolia, P16(T): Havaianas, P16(C): Havaianas, P16(B): Ocean Sole LTD; P17: Dr Martin Kunz; P18–19(BKGRD): Shooarts/Shutterstock, P18(B): EvaKaufman/istock; P19(TR): Huang Zheng/Shutterstock, P19(B): Ambika Canroy; P20(T): Kobby Dagan/Shutterstock, P20(BL): 2014 Turtle Doves Ltd, P20(BR): TongChuwit/Shutterstock; P21(R): 2014 Peruvian Connection; P20–21(BKGRD): Shooarts/Shutterstock, P21(BR): Joel Shawn/Shutterstock; P22(C): AMA/Shutterstock, P22(BKGRD): HomeArt/Shutterstock; P23(T): Michael S. Yamashita/Corbis, P23(CT): TongChuwit/Shutterstock, P23(B): Dr. Morley Read/Shutterstock, P24–25(BKGRD): HomeArt/Shutterstock, P24(T): Pete Niesen/Shutterstock; P25(T): Suvra Kanti Das/Zuma Press/Corbis, P25(B): Studio Veja; P26: Fuyu Liu/Shutterstock; P26–27(BKGRD): Madlen/Shutterstock, P27(T): Dmitry Naumov/Shutterstock, P27(B): Elena Mirage/Shutterstock; P28(T): Robert Harding Picture Library Ltd/Alamy, P28(B): Jackiso/Shutterstock, P29(BL) TongChuwit/Shutterstock, P29(T): Papilio/Alamy, P29(C): Teresa Levite/Shutterstock, P29(BR): Nomads Clothing; P30–31: Malgorzata Kistryn/Shutterstock; P32: Malgorzata Kistryn/Shutterstock.
Illustrations: all-free-downloads.com (P6–7(BKGRD), 9(BKGRD), 26–27(BKGRD), 28–29(BKGRD)).

Library and Archives Canada Cataloguing in Publication

Greathead, Helen, author
     My t-shirt and other clothing / Helen Greathead.

(Well made, fair trade)
Includes index.
Issued in print and electronic formats.
ISBN 978-0-7787-2716-3 (hardback).--
ISBN 978-0-7787-2739-2 (paperback).--
ISBN 978-1-4271-1820-2 (html)

     1. Clothing trade--Juvenile literature. 2. Clothing trade--Moral and ethical aspects--Juvenile literature. 3. Clothing workers--Juvenile literature. I. Title.

HD9940.A2G74 2016   j381'.45687   C2016-902583-7
                                                                                      C2016-902584-5

Library of Congress Cataloging-in-Publication Data

CIP available at the Library of Congress

R0446784604

Contents

Why buy fair trade?   4

Cotton T-shirts   6

Denim jeans   10

Flip-flops   14

Soft sweaters   18

Sneakers   22

Silk   26

Glossary   30

Websites   31

Index   32

Words in **bold** can be found in the glossary on page 30.

Why buy fair trade?

Many people work making the clothing and shoes we buy at stores. Fair trade organizations, such as the Fairtrade Foundation, help ensure that everyone involved in making clothing, from the farmer who grows the plants that fabrics are made from to the garment worker who sews the clothing, is treated fairly.

Fair trade organizations encourage clothing companies to produce clothes that are kind to the environment and to the people who make them.

What is fair trade?

Most of the clothes we buy are produced in **developing countries**, such as India and China. Often, the people who work in fields and factories where the materials for our clothes are sourced and put together, are paid very little and have poor working conditions. Fair trade organizations try to ensure workers are paid a fair price for the work they do and that their working conditions are not dangerous.

Labeling fashion

Not many clothing items come with a fair trade label yet. But clothing with the labels FAIRTRADE, World Fair Trade Organization, or Fair Wear Foundation, mean that the items were produced according to fair trade standards.

FAIRTRADE
Certified Cotton

Look for fair trade marks and labels, such as this FAIRTRADE Mark, on clothing and footwear when you go shopping.

Fair trade schemes

This book describes some of the problems faced by people in the developing world, who make or provide the **raw materials** for many of our clothes. It explains some fair trade solutions, and will help you to understand why fair trade is so important and how you can help by being careful about where you shop and what you buy.

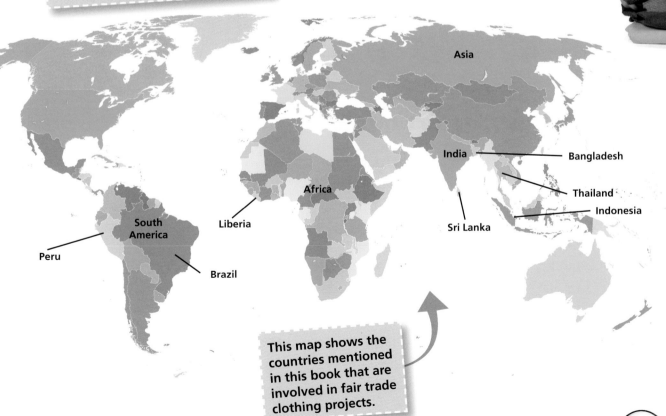

Asia

India — Bangladesh

Africa — Thailand

Liberia — Indonesia

South America — Sri Lanka

Peru

Brazil

This map shows the countries mentioned in this book that are involved in fair trade clothing projects.

Cotton T-shirts

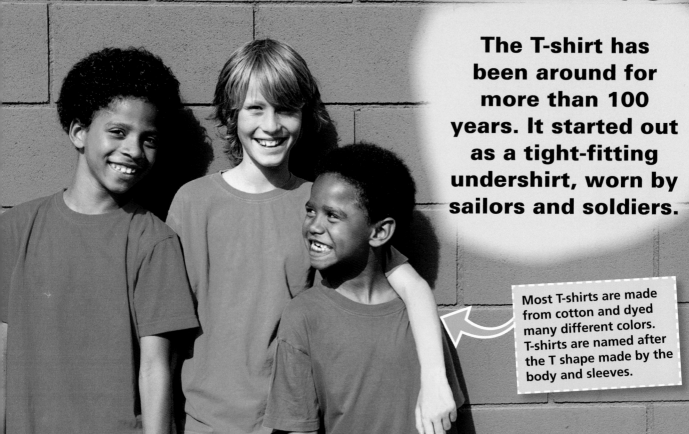

The T-shirt has been around for more than 100 years. It started out as a tight-fitting undershirt, worn by sailors and soldiers.

Most T-shirts are made from cotton and dyed many different colors. T-shirts are named after the T shape made by the body and sleeves.

How is your T-shirt made?

The cotton plant takes about 200 days to grow. Its boll, or seed, splits open, and fibers that look like cotton balls burst out. Cotton is **harvested** by hand or machine. Seeds inside the cotton are separated and used to make cottonseed oil, while the raw cotton fiber is sent to a textile mill. There, it is pulled, stretched, and twisted into yarn, then dyed to make the cotton fabric for clothing such as T-shirts. The fabric is sewn into garments in a factory, often in India or China.

Where does cotton come from?

Cotton grows in warm climates all around the world. China, India, the United States, and Uzbekistan in central Asia, are the largest producers of cotton. In many developing countries, such as India and parts of Africa and South America, cotton is still picked by hand, mainly by women and children. The pickers are often poorly paid and many live in **poverty**.

Chemical dangers

Cotton plants are often treated with large amounts of **pesticide** to prevent them from being damaged by insects and diseases. However, chemicals in the pesticides can cause headaches, sickness, and breathing difficulties for the workers who apply them.

Pesticides that have been banned in **developed countries** such as the United States and Canada, because they are dangerous to human and animal health, are sometimes still sold to developing countries for use in cotton fields. Workers who spray the pesticides often have no training or protective equipment. These pesticides run off the fields when it rains and contaminate nearby streams and rivers. This is harmful to the environment.

Environment matters

Non-organic cotton farming uses nearly a quarter of all the world's **insecticides** and about 10 percent of the world's pesticides. Environmental groups, such as the Pesticide Action Network and the Toxics Action Center, encourage farmers to use **non-toxic** pesticides. This is not only better for the environment, the wildlife, and the health of farm workers, it is also cheaper. Many toxic pesticides are expensive to buy and farmers must use a large amount on their crops.

In many countries, cotton is picked by women and children. These children are picking cotton in Uzbekistan.

Case study: Agrocel, India

The Ranchhod family lives on a small cotton farm in Gujarat in western India. Growing cotton is hard, especially at harvest time, when work starts at 6 a.m. and there's hardly a break until 4 p.m. Khima Ranchhod sells his cotton through Fairtrade to Agrocel, a **cooperative** that encourages local workers to produce **organic**, Fairtrade cotton. Khima and his family earn a better price for their crop now, because the cooperative sells the cotton to buyers in the developed world. Today, Khima's cotton can be found in products made for companies such as the British department store Marks & Spencer.

Low costs, high profits

Agrocel has helped Khima to become an organic grower and shown him how to keep his production costs low. With higher profits, Khima can now afford to buy organic fertilizer such as manure to help the cotton grow. Water is scarce, but manure helps keep moisture in the soil. Khima and his wife Jamnaben hope they will soon have enough money to send their daughters to school, and perhaps put a tiled roof on their house.

Organic farming means that fewer chemical pesticides are sprayed on the cotton plants. This means workers who pick the cotton by hand are less likely to become ill.

Reuse, recycle

What can you do with a tired old T-shirt? You can donate it to a **clothing bank,** give it to a charity shop—or you can cut off the sleeves, deepen the neck and sew up the bottom of the T-shirt to make a colorful bag!

Good buy!

Rapanui calls itself an eco-fashion company. It was set up in 2008, by brothers Rob and Mart Drake-Knight. All Rapanui T-shirts are made in India, using handpicked organic cotton that is transported by camel and cart to a factory powered by wind energy. The company uses fair trade and Fair Wear suppliers, so they know that the people who provide their cotton have been paid fairly and that the cotton production has not damaged the environment.

This T-shirt is a tribute to the work done by Sea Shepherd, a group that protects whales.

Rapanui designed this T-shirt to support the Marine Conservation Society (MCS). They give 50 percent of all profits made on these T-shirts to the MCS.

Denim jeans

Around the world, the market for denim jeans is projected to reach $56 billion by 2018. Around 17 percent of all cotton produced is made into denim.

The first jeans

The first jeans were made from a thick, heavy material used for tents and wagon covers during the **gold rush** in California in the 1850s. They were intended as strong, hard-wearing work clothes for farmers, miners, and cowboys. The denim company Levi Strauss produced the first jeans with **rivets** in 1873. They were designed to be even stronger and less likely to rip. They were produced in blue denim, canvas, and brown duck (a heavy cotton material).

The world's oldest surviving pair of Levi's jeans. They date back to 1879 and are called buckle-backs. These jeans have been valued at around $126,084.

Rivets are permanent metal fasteners used to strengthen jeans. They are usually found at the corners and sides of the pockets to hold the fabric together where it is too thick to be sewn.

Where do your jeans come from?

Today, cotton could be picked in the United States, then flown to India to be made into fabric. Thread may come from Turkey or Hungary, with dyes from Spain, and a zipper made in Japan (with the brass coming from zinc and copper mined in Australia or Namibia). Buttons made in China or Africa might be added to the final garment.

How are jeans made?

Denim fabric is woven from two cotton yarns. One is dyed indigo blue, which shows on the outside, and the other is white, which shows on the inside. The fabric is cut into shaped pieces, which are put together by hand, then sewn together on special sewing machines. Zippers, pockets, and rivets are added, and seams and hems stitched up. The jeans are then washed to fade the denim and tagged for shipping to stores.

A survey found that, on average, people in the U.S. have seven pairs of jeans in their wardrobe.

Working conditions

Some jeans are **sandblasted** to make them look worn and faded. This process can lead to health problems for factory workers. The dust from the sand can get into workers' lungs, and over time cause a deadly disease called silicosis. Silicosis causes breathing problems and bad coughs. Factories rarely provide health care or protective clothing. In 2012, the Clean Clothes Campaign, a group that works to improve conditions for garment workers, called on manufacturers to stop sandblasting by changing the designs of their jeans. They **petitioned** fashion companies to ban sandblasting on their garments altogether, and to ask local workers' organizations to make sure factories followed this ban. Many jean companies, including Benetton, Gucci, H&M, and Levi Strauss & Co. have agreed.

Many jeans are made in overcrowded factories in countries such as Bangladesh, Turkey, and China, where pay is low and shifts can last for up to 12 hours a day.

Good buy!

A company called Kuyichi was set up in 2001 after its Dutch founders could not persuade large fashion manufacturers to switch to organic cotton. The company makes jeans using organic cotton and natural dyes that do not risk workers' health. The water in their factories is cleaned and recycled. Kuyichi is a member of the Fair Wear Foundation.

Kuyichi makes jeans from recycled denim as well as organic cotton.

Case study: Rana Plaza, Dhaka, Bangladesh

Nasima Begum worked in the Rana Plaza factory sewing up jeans. One day, after a crack appeared in the walls of the factory building, her bosses sent her home. She was terrified, but returned to work the next day on her bosses' orders. Her whole family relied on her earnings of $110 a month and she was scared of losing her job. Sadly, the building collapsed and Nasima's body was never found.

Nasima's family was devastated by her loss. They have also not been able to claim any **compensation**. Some international clothing companies have paid compensation to the workers and their families, but this is not required because they are not held responsible for the accident. The Rana Plaza Donors Trust, set up by the Clean Clothes Campaign, distributed $30 million in compensation and is pushing for a workplace injury plan in Bangladesh.

Back to school

Verité-Sheva is a Bangladeshi program that encourages children affected by the building collapse to stay in school. Many worked to earn money to help support their families. By providing two good meals a day in school, many children are now able to return to school and study. The program also encourages safety in the workplace, and is teaching health and safety to managers in some of the largest clothing companies. Verité-Sheva is supported by some international clothing makers and stores.

More than 2,200 workers were pulled alive from the wreckage of Rana Plaza, but over 1,000 died. Many survivors were badly injured and are now disabled.

Flip-flops

Flip-flops are cheap to mass-produce and are worn by millions of people around the world. In many developing countries, flip-flops might be the only shoes people own.

What are flip-flops made of?

Flip-flops can be made from many different materials, but most have plastic straps and natural or **synthetic** rubber soles. Synthetic rubber is produced from oil, but natural rubber comes from trees grown in **plantations** in countries such as Thailand, Vietnam, Sri Lanka, Liberia, and Guatemala.

Flip-flops became popular in the U.S. after World War II, when returning soldiers brought traditional zori and geta sandals from Japan.

How is rubber produced?

Each morning, in a rubber plantation, the trees are cut so that the sap, or latex, trickles out into a cup attached to the tree. This is called tapping. Workers collect the latex, mix it with acid, and roll it through a machine to form a sheet.

Plantation workers in developing countries in Africa and South-east Asia often live in housing supplied by the plantation owners, without running water or electricity.

Latex is a white liquid that is tapped from trees and used to make rubber.

Case study: Harbel, Liberia, Africa

In Liberia, workers on rubber plantations worked 12-hour shifts for low wages, and were sometimes ordered to double their production for no extra pay. Each worker was expected to tap up to 800 trees in a shift, and carry buckets of latex weighing 66 pounds (30 kg) each for 1.5 miles (2.4 km) to the weighing station. Sometimes workers brought their children to help, because they could not get the job done without them.

Union agreement

In 2010, an agreement was signed between the Firestone Natural Rubber Company and the employees' union. The agreement banned children from working on the plantations, reduced the amount of latex employees were expected to collect, and provided better systems of transportation.

Before the agreement, workers carried heavy buckets of latex to be weighed. Today, tractors and trucks carry the latex to the weighing station.

Fair trade flip-flops

The Havaianas factory in Brazil started making flip-flops in 1962 and is now the largest manufacturer of flip-flops in the world, making an average of six pairs a second. The Havaianas factory follows many fair trade practices and donates money to the Institute for Ecological Studies, which helps to protect the environment in Brazil. The company has also given money to build sports facilities to help keep children and young people involved in healthy activities.

Havaianas in Brazil produces 184 million pairs of flip-flops a year.

Good buy!

Thousands of old flip-flops wash up on the beaches of Kenya, East Africa, every year, ruining the beach and harming coastal wildlife. After some local people began using the flip-flops to make children's toys, they eventually formed a company called Ocean Sole. Now they sell recycled flip-flop products around the world.

Environment matters

In Kerala, south-western India, a company called Guru makes traditional Indian-designed flip-flops. They use natural rubber from their own farms and plant a tree for every pair sold. If you throw away old Guru flip-flops, they break down naturally and don't harm the environment.

Case study: Frocester Rubber Plantation, Sri Lanka

Madhura is 10 years old and she has lived all her life on the Frocester rubber plantation where her parents work. Madhura's family are Tamil, a **minority** group in Sri Lanka that experiences **discrimination**. The government even refused to supply them with electricity. Luckily, Frocester is a fair trade plantation.

Electricity supplies

The workers there receive a premium from the rubber they produce, which is given back to the workers' community. In 2011, money earned from fair trade allowed plantation workers to have their own electricity supply installed. Now Madhura can do her homework and iron her school uniform after dark.

Fair trade is helping Madhura to get a better education, which might mean she can earn enough to help support her family when she is older.

Soft sweaters

We all know that wool comes from sheep, but did you know that your softest sweater could be made from rabbit fur or wool from an alpaca?

Where does angora come from?

Angora rabbits originally come from Turkey. Today, Chinese farms and factories keep around 50 million angora rabbits, providing 90 percent of the world's yearly production of 2,755 to 3,306 tons (2,500 to 3,000 metric tons) of angora wool. Some of the wool is **exported** for processing in Europe and Japan. Angora rabbits are also farmed in Argentina, Chile, the Czech Republic, and Hungary.

Angora wool comes from rabbits, while angora goats produce mohair. Wool from angora rabbits is 800 percent warmer than wool from sheep.

How is angora produced?

Angora rabbits need regular grooming to stop their fur from matting. They **molt** naturally every three months and at that stage their fur can be gently plucked by hand or sheared. Recent reports have shown that rabbits in some factories live in terrible conditions. The animals are kept in tiny, dirty cages that are rarely cleaned out. The wire on the bottom of the cage can cut their feet, and they are given no space to run and play. To speed up collection, the rabbits' fur is collected in a way that hurts the rabbits and leaves them shocked and in pain. A healthy angora rabbit can live up to ten years, but most farmed rabbits die within two years.

In 2013, the animal rights organization PETA (People for the **Ethical** Treatment of Animals) exposed these conditions, and top retail stores such as H&M and Esprit stopped selling angora products. Twelve clothing companies have now banned angora products from being used in their clothing and accessories.

Angora rabbits have different-colored fur, from white, tan, and gray to brown and black. Many garments made from their wool use these natural colors but for some garments the wool is dyed different colors.

Good buy!

Ambika Conroy keeps her own rabbits on her farm in New York State. She gently shears the rabbits' fur every three months, then spins and knits it into hats, scarves, sweaters, jackets, and legwarmers to sell through her website.

Some of Ambika Conroy's products made from the wool from her angora rabbits.

Alpacas have been bred in South America for thousands of years. Although it is similar to sheep's wool, alpaca wool is warmer, naturally water-repellant, and more fire resistant.

Alpaca farmers in Peru

We also get wool for soft sweaters from alpacas. Alpaca farmers in the Peruvian Andes are poor and there is little education available because they live in such a remote area. Today, help for the herders comes from Pacomarca, a company that supports **sustainable** alpaca farming. Pacomarca provides training in the latest shearing techniques, and animal health and breeding. It also helps to train farmers in house-building and supports local schools and teaching. In addition, a group called Inca Tops has donated wool and set up textile workshops for mothers in small mountain villages to teach them how to knit sweaters for sale.

Good buy!

Turtle Doves, based in Shropshire, United Kingdom, makes accessories, such as fingerless gloves and scarves, out of old sweaters. Turtle Dove products are sold mainly online. Susan Harris Design in Toronto also makes clothing out of recycled old sweaters, such as mitts, hats, and skirts.

Reuse, recycle

It's easy to recycle an old wool sweater by unpicking the yarn and reusing it. You can even buy recycled wool on eBay that has been unraveled for you. Then you can learn to knit your own wooly items, such as a scarf or mittens.

Case study: Peruvian Connection, USA

This alpaca cardigan comes from an American company called Peruvian Connection. Company founders, Biddy and Anne Hurlbut, have been importing alpaca products from Peru since 1976. The company's sweaters and cardigans are made by Peruvian workers who are paid a good price for their work, and given bonuses, hot meals, and help with transportation and childcare.

Local projects

Peruvian Connection supports many local projects, including an orphanage and a program for teaching disabled children. It also supports Pro Mujer in Peru, an organization which enables women to operate small businesses by helping them find loans, business training, and affordable healthcare.

Dyed alpaca yarn. Alpaca wool is softer and warmer than sheep's wool.

Peruvian Connection garments are all made by skilled Peruvian workers.

Sneakers

Around 350 million sports shoes are sold every year in the United States alone. You don't have to play a sport to wear sneakers, but once your shoes have worn out, recycle them—they could be turned into a new sports track!

Today, many sports have their own sports-specific shoes.

Fair trade for feet

When it comes to fair trade, there is a long way to go in the footwear industry, from getting a good deal for employees making shoes in factories to protecting the rights of animals that are mistreated in the production of cheap leather. Independent companies are making a difference, but there is still a long way to go to improve conditions for everyone involved in the **supply chain.** Many people still work long hours in unsafe conditions and are poorly paid.

Where do sneakers come from?

Large, well-known footwear companies often use factories in China, India, Cambodia, Vietnam, the Philippines, and Indonesia to make their shoes. Manufacturers like to produce sneakers and runners in these countries because factory production is cheap. Employers are often not required by law to ensure worker health and safety, so production costs are low.

How are sneakers made?

Making sneakers is a complicated business, and producing the sole is particularly difficult. It could have three layers: an insole; a midsole with a core of gel, foam, liquid **silicone**, or even compressed air; and an outsole made of rubber.

The upper, or top part, of the sneakers might be canvas, synthetic fabric, or leather, cut to shape with holes punched for the laces, then stitched together. The heel and toe are stiffened before the upper is heated and molded into shape. The sole is attached to the upper, and laces are added by hand.

Workers in China check finished sneakers as they roll past on a conveyor belt.

In some countries, patches of rain forest are burnt and cleared so they can be used as grazing land for cattle. Cattle skins are used to create the leather for making sneakers and other shoes.

Reuse, recycle

VivoBarefoot shoes make the nylon that covers their sneakers from recycled plastic bottles. The soles are made from natural latex and rice husks, and the insoles are non-toxic, **biodegradable** gel pads. Even the shoe tree that holds the shape of the shoe is made from recycled cardboard.

In Fez, Morocco, people have been tanning leather with natural dyes for over 1,000 years. This **tannery** uses vats full of different colored dyes.

Processing leather

Leather is animal skin that has been through a process called tanning. Tanning makes the animal skin clean and strong so it can be used for clothing, shoes, and bags. However, unprotected workers can suffer from the chemicals that are used in the tanning process. One substance, **chromium**, has been linked to cancer, asthma, bronchitis, and pneumonia. It is a problem for workers in some Indian, Pakistani, and South American tanning factories. In addition, dangerous chemical waste has been found flowing out of the factories. Chromium in the waste can **contaminate** nearby soil, and food that grows in the soil. It can also pollute local drinking water, endangering the people and animals that drink it, as well as the fish that live in it.

Environment matters

The Blacksmith Institute is an international **non-governmental organization** (NGO) that focuses on finding solutions to the problems of toxic waste. Their researchers have found ways of cleaning up toxic chromium by treating it either with another type of chromium, or with charcoal from burned animal bones. After treating **groundwater** from 300 tanneries around Kanpur in India, some wells were tested and showed hardly any trace of chromium.

Case study: Tanning factories in Hazaribagh, Bangladesh

Leather factories are booming in Bangladesh because labor is cheap. Around 15,000 people work in the 150 tanning factories of Hazaribagh. They work without eye protection or facemasks, using dangerous chemicals such as chromium.

Burning skin

At one **tannery**, 17-year-old Jahad says acid in the water makes his skin burn. He suffers from asthma and has rashes on his body, but he has to work at the factory because there are no other jobs available.

Now the factory has plans to move to a new building, where working conditions will be much better. This is as a result of the Rana Plaza disaster (see page 13), which has put pressure on international manufacturers to improve working conditions in Bangladesh.

These workers are soaking animal skins in baths of water mixed with chemicals. They wear very little protective clothing.

Good buy!

Veja's fair trade sneakers cost three to four times more to produce than ordinary sneakers, but the company saves money by not advertising. The shoes sell by word of mouth.

The French company Veja makes its sneakers in Brazil. The canvas uppers are made from organic fair trade cotton, and fair trade rubber is used for the soles. Fair trade leather is harder to source. Veja is careful where its leather comes from, and is working to improve its supply chain.

Silk

It may be hard to believe, but beautiful soft silk is made from the cocoons of caterpillars. Thousands of cocoons are needed to make one simple dress.

It takes about 3,000 silkworm cocoons to make 17.6 ounces (500 g) of silk. It would take 5,000 cocoons to make one silk robe.

Where is silk produced?

A Chinese legend tells how silk was discovered in 2640 B.C.E., when a silkworm cocoon fell into Empress Si Ling Chi's hot cup of tea and started to unravel. The empress twisted the fibers together and wove it into fabric.

Today, silk is produced in more than 60 countries around the world. Most silk still comes from China, which produces three times more silk than India, the next biggest producer. Silk comes from other countries, too, such as Thailand, Uzbekistan, Brazil, and Vietnam.

How is silk made?

Bombyx mori silkworms are a type of caterpillar. After the caterpillars hatch, they eat a lot of mulberry leaves and grow to 10,000 times the size they were at birth in about 30-40 days. Then the silkworm takes three days to build a cocoon while it turns into a moth. The cocoon is then boiled and the silk thread is unraveled. One cocoon will provide a strand of thread around 1,640 feet (500 m) long. The strands are dyed and woven by hand or machine to make silk fabric.

Millions of silkworm cocoons grow in baskets at silkworm farms.

Problems with production

Workers in silk mills can develop lung infections, caused by fine dust that comes from the fabric. The longer a worker stays in the same job, the higher the chances they will become ill. In Mumbai, India, one survey found that 30 percent of workers in spinning, winding, and **carding** departments had breathing difficulties.

Dyes and chemicals used to color the fabric can also cause rashes and sickness. Possible solutions to these problems include keeping dust levels low and giving workers protective clothing to wear. At the moment, there are no fair trade programs set up to help workers in bigger factories, but some smaller, independent companies are finding better ways to work.

The effects of the dust in silk mills can be reduced if workers wear facemasks and move around the mill doing different jobs.

Case study: Sawang Boran, Thailand

Sawang Boran means "ancient brilliance" in the Thai language. The project, which was set up in 2008, encourages young women to learn traditional silk-weaving techniques that will help them to earn a living. An elderly woman named Yaa Lai, and other local weavers are teaching valuable skills to younger workers. By selling their fabrics and silk products around the world, the women are turning silk-making into a business. Profits from the sale of their silk products are put back into the project.

This young girl is weaving silk on a loom in the traditional way.

Fair trade, fair price

Through the Sawang Boran project, women are trained and given interest-free loans to start their businesses and buy equipment, such as looms and sewing machines.

The project holds regular meetings where the women can share skills and discuss ideas and problems, as well as calculate their earnings. They are paid a fair price for their silk and work a maximum of 5–6 hours a day, leaving time for them to spend with their children and families.

Before the project began, the women used synthetic dyes and chemical bleaches. Now all their dyes and silk are organic.

Good buy!

Silk made by the Masuta **collective** in India comes from tussah silkworms that live wild in the forest. These silkworms transform into moths and leave the cocoon before the silk is collected. The collective was set up to help poor women find work. Now, 2,500 women are producing tussah silk. The women had training in how to rear silkworms; trees were planted to feed the caterpillars and netting was put up to protect them.

Tussah silkworms eat oak leaves. A substance called tannin in the leaves makes the silk naturally honey-colored. Tussah silk yarn is thicker than mulberry silk. It can be dyed and made into fabric for clothes.

Reuse, recycle

In India, at the time of the August full moon, girls traditionally throw out their old saris and their brothers give them a new one. Online retailer Nomads Clothing sells a line of clothing made from these recycled silk saris. This company has been producing fair trade clothes for 20 years to help people from poorer communities support themselves.

Silk is lightweight but hard-wearing. It is warm in winter and cool in summer.

Glossary

biodegradable A material that can be broken down naturally by living things

carding Brushing or combing wool or other fiber to make it smooth before spinning

chromium A shiny metallic element

collective A group of usually small, local companies that work together

compensation Money given to workers by a company or government to help them cope with the results of an accident at work

contaminate To pollute with a poisonous substance

cooperative A group of people, or organizations, working together and sharing any benefits or profits evenly between them

developed countries Countries that are wealthy, industrialized, and have a high standard of living

developing countries Countries where most people are not well off, but local resources are being used to build up different industries

discrimination The unjust treatment of people based on race, religion, gender, age, or abilities

ethical The right thing to do, such as paying workers a fair wage even though this means less profit

export To ship goods out of a country to be sold in other parts of the world

fibers Fine threads which make up a yarn or fabric

gold rush When gold was discovered in California in 1848, thousands rushed there to search for gold, hoping to get rich quick

groundwater Water that collects under the ground and in cracks in the soil or rocks

harvested Collected crops

insecticides Sprays that stop insects and bugs from eating and damaging crops

mass produce To make a lot of one product quickly and usually cheaply in a factory

minority A small group of people, often discriminated against in a community or country

molt To shed fur ready for new fur to grow

non-governmental organization A group that provides services or advocates on behalf of people, but does not belong to any government

non-organic Crops sprayed with pesticides that can damage the environment and wildlife

non-toxic Something that will not damage the environment, harm wildlife, or make people ill

organic Crops which are produced without using chemicals

pesticide A chemical used to prevent insects and diseases from damaging crops

petition A request for change that is signed by people and sent to a large organization or government

plantation Huge area of the same sort of plants grown for a single crop

poverty Being very poor and not having enough money or resources for daily needs

premium An extra payment on top of the normal price for goods

raw materials The basic (unprocessed) materials that are used to make a product

rivet A small metal plate used to hold traditional jeans together

sandblast Apply a jet of sand powered by air or steam to roughen or clean something

silicone A tough, artificial substance used to make rubber and plastics

supply chain The journey of an object from the sourcing of materials to when it reaches the stores

synthetic A human-made material created through a chemical process to imitate a natural material

tannery A place where animal skins and hides are processed and turned into leather

Websites

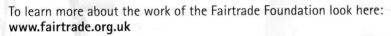

To learn more about the work of the Fairtrade Foundation look here:
www.fairtrade.org.uk

For how to turn your T-shirt into a shopping bag look here:
www.instructables.com/id/FASTEST-RECYCLED-T-SHIRT-TOTE-BAG

Find out more about Rapanui, how they started, the organizations they support, and the clothes they make here: **www.rapanuiclothing.com/about.html**

Find out more about Ocean Sole flip-flop products here: **www.ocean-sole.com**

Read about the Clean Clothes Campaign here: **www.cleanclothes.org**

To find out more about Kuyichi Jeans, including how to buy them, look here:
www.kuyichi.com

To find out more about the Fair Wear Foundation and the companies that are members, check here: **www.fairwear.org**

See angora collected in an animal-friendly way:
http://thekidshouldseethis.com/post/69074981856

Find things to do with your old sweaters here:
www.youtube.com/watch?v=WyZKq63447w

Find out more about the policy behind Nomads Clothing: **http://www.nomadsclothing.com/fair-trade-policy**

Learn more about the organizations that the Havaianas company helps here:
http://en-gb.havaianas.com/en-GB/responsibility/

Index

Agrocel 8
alpacas 20–21
angora rabbits 18–19

Bangladesh 5, 11, 12, 13, 25
Blacksmith Institute 24
Brazil 5, 16, 25

children working 6, 7, 15
China 4, 6, 11, 12,18, 22, 23, 26
chromium 24
Clean Clothes Campaign 12, 13
Conroy, Ambika 19
cotton 6–9, 11

developing countries 4, 5, 7

education 13, 17, 20, 21

factories 4, 12, 13, 18, 22, 23,
    24, 25, 27
fair trade 4
Fairtrade Foundation 4, 5, 9
Fair Wear Foundation 5, 9, 12
farmers 7, 20
flip-flops 14–17
Frocester Rubber Plantation 17

ill health 7, 12, 24, 25, 26, 27
India 4, 5, 6, 8, 9, 22, 24, 27, 29
    Kerala 5, 16
Indonesia 5
insecticides 7

jeans 10-13

Kuyichi 12

latex 15, 23
leather 22, 24, 25
Liberia 5, 15

Morocco 24

Ocean Sole 16
organic farming 8, 9, 12, 25

Peru 5, 20, 21
Pesticide Action Network (PAN UK) 7
pesticides 7, 8
PETA (People for the Ethical Treatment
    of Animals) 19
plantations 14–15
pollution 7, 24
poverty 6, 14, 15, 17, 21, 28

rain forest 23
Rana Plaza 13
Rapanui 9
recycling 9, 12, 16, 20, 23, 29
rubber 14, 15, 16, 17

Sawang Boran project 28
silicosis 12
silk 26–29
sneakers 22-23
Soil Association 7
South America 4, 6, 24
Sri Lanka 5, 17
sweaters 18-21

T-shirts 6-9
tanning leather 24, 25
Thailand 5, 26, 28
toxic waste 24
Turkey 12
Turtle Doves 20

United States 6, 10, 19, 22
Uzbekistan 6, 7, 26

Veja 25
VivoBarefoot 23

wool, alpaca 20-21
wool, angora 18-19
World Fair Trade Organization
    (WFTO) 5